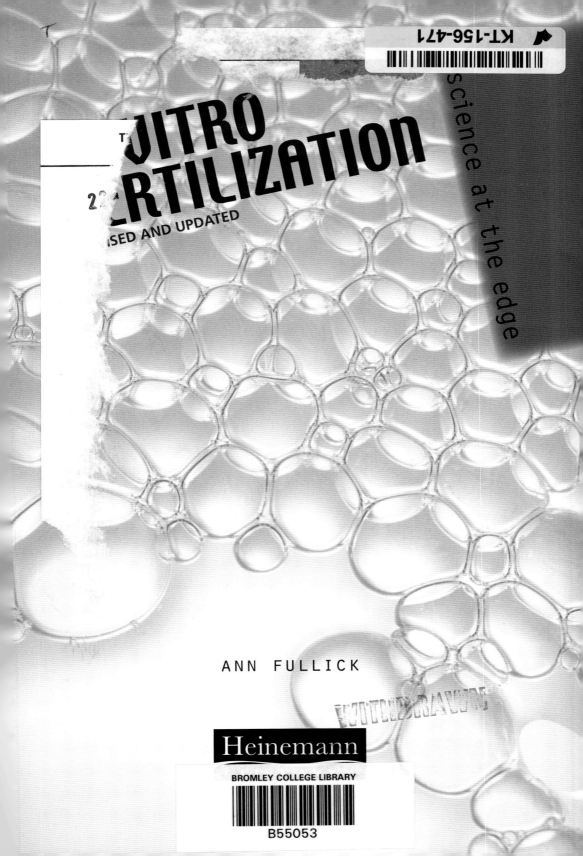

IN VITRO
FERTILIZATION

REVISED AND UPDATED

science at the edge

ANN FULLICK

Heinemann

www.heinemann.co.uk/library
Visit our website to find out more information about **Heinemann Library** books.

To order:

☎ Phone 44 (0) 1865 888066

📄 Send a fax to 44 (0) 1865 314091

💻 Visit the Heinemann Bookshop at www.heinemann.co.uk/library to browse our catalogue and order online.

Heinemann Library is an imprint of Capstone Global Library Limited, a company incorporated in England and Wales having its registered office at 7 Pilgrim Street, London, EC4V 6LB – Registered company number: 6695582

"Heinemann" is a registered trademark of Pearson Education Limited, under licence to Capstone Global Library Limited

Edited by Pollyanna Poulter and Claire Throp
Designed by Philippa Jenkins and Artistix
Original illustrations © Capstone Global Library
    Limited by Art Construction
Picture research by Ruth Blair
Production by Victoria Fitzgerald
Originated by Chroma Graphics (Overseas) Pte. Ltd
Printed and bound in China by South China Printing
    Company Ltd.

ISBN 978 0 431124 90 2 (hardback)
13 12 11 10 09
10 9 8 7 6 5 4 3 2 1

ISBN 978 0 431149 44 8 (paperback)
13 12 11 10 09
10 9 8 7 6 5 4 3 2 1

British Library Cataloguing-in-Publication Data
Fullick, Ann, 1956-
In vitro fertilization. - 2nd ed. - (Science at the edge)
1. Fertilization in vitro, Human - Juvenile literature
2. Fertilization in vitro, Human - Moral and ethical aspects - Juvenile literature
I. Title
618.1'78'0599
A full catalogue record for this book is available from the British Library.

Acknowledgements
We would like to thank the following for permission to reproduce photographs: © Associated Press p. **50**; © CARE at the Park p. **38**; © Corbis pp. **17** (Patrick Bennett), **41** (Bogdan Cristel/Reuters), **49** (Cindy Yamanaka/Orange County Register), **53** (Scott T. Smith); © Doriver Lilley pp. **36**, **39**; © Getty Images pp. **43** (News), **23** (Popperfoto); © Mary Evans Picture Library p. **18**; © PA Photos pp. **32** (PA Archive/Andrew Parsons), **54** (AP Photo/Antonio Calanni), **57** (PA Archive/Andrew Parsons), **55**; © Photolibrary Group p. **30** (Digital Vision); © Photoshot p. **10** (Tetra Images); © Rex Features p. **22**; © Sally & Richard Greenhill p. **12**; © Science Photo Library pp. **4** (Stevie Grand), **7** (Prof. P. Motta/Dept. of anatomy/University "La Sapienza", Rome), **9** (Bettina Salomon), **13**, **14**, **21** (Dr Yorgos Nikas), **25** (Mauro Fermariello), **26** (Living Art Enterprises, LLC), **27** (AJ Photo), **28** (Dr Yorgos Nikas), **42** (Hank Morgan), **45** and **48** (James King-Holmes); © Topham Picturepoint p. **43**.

Cover photograph of petri dish with eggs reproduced with permission of © Science Photo Library/Mauro Fermariello.

We would like to thank Richard Howell for his invaluable help in the preparation of this book.

Every effort has been made to contact copyright holders of material reproduced in this book. Any omissions will be rectified in subsequent printings if notice is given to the Publishers.

CONTENTS

Some words are printed in bold, **like this**. You can find out what they mean by looking in the glossary.

AN EVERYDAY MIRACLE?

Every moment of every day a baby is born somewhere around the world. Each new human being comes into existence as the result of the joining of two minute cells from the parents to form a single new cell. It is this cell that then grows and divides to form the billions of cells that make up the body of a newborn baby.

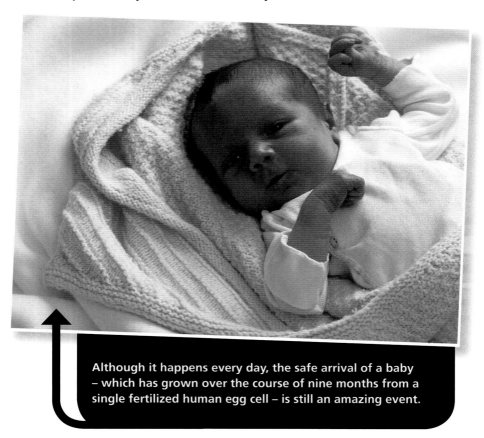

Although it happens every day, the safe arrival of a baby – which has grown over the course of nine months from a single fertilized human egg cell – is still an amazing event.

What is infertility?

For lots of people, having babies is very easy. There is a time each month when, if a couple have sexual intercourse, there is a chance that an **ovum** (egg) in the body of the woman will be **fertilized** by a **sperm** from the man and nine months later a baby will be born. In fact, many people spend years trying to avoid pregnancy, using different methods of **contraception**. But what happens if pregnancy and babies don't happen when they *are* wanted?

The lives of many ordinary people have been blighted by the inability to have a much-wanted child. Although there are many different causes of **infertility**, for centuries the solutions were few and far between – adopting a child or becoming resigned to childlessness were the main options.

So what can we do about it today? In the last 50 years, it has become increasingly possible to treat and overcome at least some forms of infertility. A wide variety of options are now available for couples who cannot produce a child naturally. These range from simple tests that make it possible to pinpoint when a woman is most likely to get pregnant, to complex techniques such as *in vitro* fertilization (IVF). This is a form of treatment where an egg and sperm are brought together outside the mother's body. They are usually mixed in a glass **Petri dish**, hence the name *in vitro* fertilization – *in vitro* is Latin for "in glass". The developing **embryo** is then replaced in the mother's body. The development of IVF has resulted in the births of thousands of babies around the world to people who would otherwise have had no hope of becoming pregnant. IVF has led the way for the development of other methods to help couples have babies. These include injecting a single sperm into an egg before placing it back in the mother's body, and freezing embryos, eggs, and ovarian tissue that – when thawed – can produce healthy babies.

Like most scientific breakthroughs, our increased ability to control human **fertility** is something of a mixed blessing. It can bring great personal happiness to couples who would otherwise be unable to have a child. At the same time it also opens up many questions about embryos that are created and then not needed, and the possibilities for changing the inherited material of an embryo before it is returned to the mother. As new and ever more sophisticated treatments for infertility are discovered, the **ethics** of each method need to be discussed. Yet the driving force behind the whole technology remains the desperate desire of infertile couples to have a child of their own.

"Every time one of my friends or family gets pregnant it hurts, but I [...] put on a smile and say my congrats. I can't wait until I'm the person in those shoes."

Member of a US Internet infertility support forum

The biology of reproduction

Young children cannot have children of their own, but as we grow and mature the parts of the body involved in making babies – technically known as **reproduction** – become active. These include the sexual organs and a gland in the brain. For many people these systems start up and run fairly smoothly, but for a growing number, things don't quite work as they should. So how does the body of a healthy, fertile woman or man work?

THE FERTILE FEMALE

For about two days in every month a woman is fertile – she has produced an egg that is mature and ready to meet a sperm. The events leading up to and following this special time form a 28-day cycle of fertility, called the **menstrual cycle**.

Inside the body of every newborn baby girl are the eggs (called ova) that will form any children she may have in the future. Once the girl goes through **puberty** the **ovaries**, which contain the eggs, become active in response to chemical signals called **hormones**.

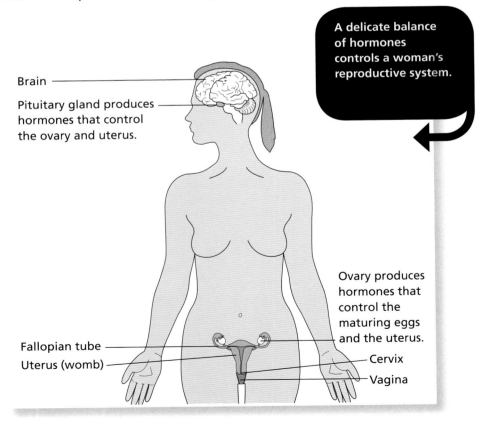

A delicate balance of hormones controls a woman's reproductive system.

Brain

Pituitary gland produces hormones that control the ovary and uterus.

Ovary produces hormones that control the maturing eggs and the uterus.

Fallopian tube

Uterus (womb)

Cervix

Vagina

Follicle Stimulating Hormone (FSH) is made by the **pituitary gland** in the brain and it has a direct effect on the ovaries. It makes some of the eggs grow and mature, ready for release. FSH also makes the ovary produce another female hormone, **oestrogen**. This triggers the build-up of the lining of the **uterus** (the organ in which the baby grows and develops) ready to nurture a pregnancy. After about fourteen days an egg is released – this is known as **ovulation** – and it leaves the ovary. The egg travels through the **Fallopian tube** towards the uterus. If it meets some sperm on the way up, it may be fertilized and a pregnancy begins. If not, the lining of the uterus gradually breaks down and passes out of the body. This is called menstruation.

REPRODUCTION IN THE MALE

Men do not have a reproductive cycle as women do, but they do have male reproductive hormones produced by the pituitary gland and by the male sex organs, the **testes**. In response to these hormones the testes make a constant supply of sperm, and other glands make the various secretions that are mixed with the sperm to form **semen**.

Whereas women usually produce a single mature egg each month, millions of sperm are produced all the time in the testes. The tails of hundreds of developing sperm can be seen here, in a tiny tube in the testes.

From conception to birth

Once a couple decide that they want a baby they need to try and make sure that sperm are present when a mature egg is released from the woman's ovary. Every time they have sexual intercourse the man releases semen containing millions of sperm into the woman's vagina. At around the same time, if the woman is at the fertile point in her menstrual cycle, an egg will be released from the ovary and begin its journey along the Fallopian tube. How do the egg and the sperm meet?

The egg cannot move – it is wafted along the Fallopian tube by the beating of millions of tiny hair-like cilia, which move it slowly away from the ovary towards the uterus. After ovulation the egg only lives for around 48 hours.

The sperm, on the other hand, have an enormously long journey to make as they travel through **mucus** and other secretions in the vagina and **cervix**, up through the uterus, and on into the Fallopian tube, which contains the egg. The journey of a single sperm can be compared to a person setting off from Britain and swimming to the United States – through treacle!

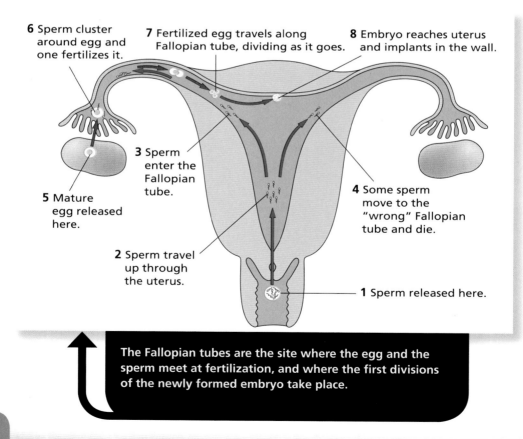

6 Sperm cluster around egg and one fertilizes it.

7 Fertilized egg travels along Fallopian tube, dividing as it goes.

8 Embryo reaches uterus and implants in the wall.

3 Sperm enter the Fallopian tube.

5 Mature egg released here.

4 Some sperm move to the "wrong" Fallopian tube and die.

2 Sperm travel up through the uterus.

1 Sperm released here.

The Fallopian tubes are the site where the egg and the sperm meet at fertilization, and where the first divisions of the newly formed embryo take place.

Each sperm makes frantic lashing movements with its tail, which keep it suspended in the liquids, and it is moved to the egg by natural muscle movements of the uterus. Some sperm reach the Fallopian tubes very quickly – in a matter of minutes – but millions are lost along the way. This is why so many sperm are produced in the first place, because the odds against any of them reaching the egg are so high!

FERTILIZATION

Once the sperm reach the egg, how is the egg actually fertilized? The sperm cluster round the egg, attracted by chemical messages it sends out. Special digestive **enzymes** in the head of the sperm act to dissolve away the protective jelly coating of the egg. Finally one sperm manages to break through and get inside the egg – after that no other sperm can get in. The nucleus of the sperm contains **genetic** information from the man while the nucleus of the egg contains genetic information from the woman. Once they fuse together, fertilization has taken place – a new genetic individual is formed and a potential new life has begun!

After fertilization the single cell begins to grow and divide as it continues to travel along the Fallopian tube to the uterus. By the time it reaches the uterus, it is a small ball of cells ready to implant in the blood-rich lining that has developed in order to support it.

Once the fertilized egg has implanted in the uterus, cell divisions, the specialization of tissue, and lots of growth take place. After nine months, a fully formed baby human being is ready to emerge and take its place in the world.

WHAT CAUSES INFERTILITY?

When a couple decide that they want to start a family and begin to try to have a baby, most expect to get pregnant straight away. After all, many of them have spent years trying very hard not to get pregnant by mistake! Even if a young, fertile couple have unprotected intercourse at the right stage of the monthly cycle there is no guarantee that they will become pregnant. The percentage chance that they will conceive gets steadily lower as they get older, and it is also reduced by lifestyle factors such as smoking, drinking, and being overweight.

For an increasing number of couples, the months without a positive pregnancy test turn into years. When infertility seems to be staring people in the face, it becomes very important to understand why pregnancy is not happening, and what, if anything, can be done about it.

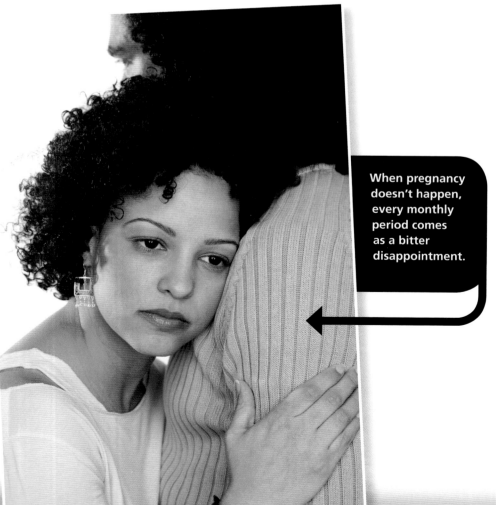

When pregnancy doesn't happen, every monthly period comes as a bitter disappointment.

Whose problem?

It is almost inevitable that, if a couple cannot have a child, they wonder whose 'fault' it is. For centuries it was assumed that childlessness was the woman's fault. We now know better! Failing to get pregnant can be the result of problems in either partner, or even both.

In about a third of all cases of infertility there is indeed a problem in the way that the body of the woman is working. However, in over a third of the cases, it is the reproductive system of the man that is not functioning as it should. The final group of infertility cases are either the result of both the man and the woman in a couple being a bit less fertile than normal or – the most puzzling of all – both partners are theoretically healthy but pregnancy just doesn't happen.

Finding out

IVF has been successful in helping to overcome some forms of infertility, but it is still a very specialized area of medicine. A couple who are having problems in conceiving a baby do not start their quest for a child with the IVF specialist – they begin with the family doctor.

Typically a doctor will check the general health of the couple in case there are any other causes of infertility not related to their reproductive systems. The doctor will also check that the woman is not taking the contraceptive pill and whether the couple are having sexual intercourse at the time of the month when the woman is most fertile. Another check will be on any other medications either partner may be taking, and whether either of them smoke or drink. Sometimes this allows the doctors to find a simple solution to fertility problems so that medical intervention is not needed for them to start a family.

For many the solution is not quite so simple, and doctors will refer a couple to an infertility specialist when it becomes apparent that they are having real difficulty in conceiving. For older couples, especially, the "biological clock" is ticking away fast, as a woman's fertility begins to fall as she approaches 40. It is important that they start working with an infertility specialist as soon as possible. However, most specialists would rather see all couples with fertility problems sooner rather than later, to try to find a successful solution to their problems.

An infertile woman ...

When a couple can't have a baby a number of different tests are carried out on both partners to try and find out the cause of the infertility, because different causes need different solutions.

OVULATION PROBLEMS

To find out why a woman is not conceiving, doctors look for both physical and chemical causes. One of the first checks will be to see if ovulation is occurring – because no egg equals no baby.

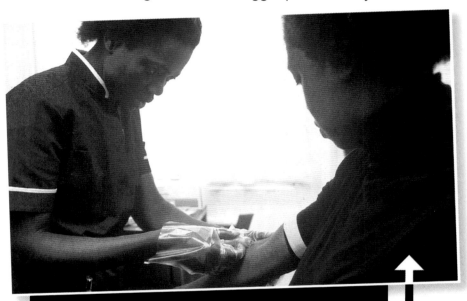

By measuring the levels of different hormones in the blood, doctors can build up a reasonably good picture of what is going on and whether ovulation is taking place.

There can be several explanations for a lack of ovulation. Sometimes the situation is very stark – there are no eggs in the ovaries. However, this is relatively rare and is the cause of infertility in only one to two per cent of the women who have difficulty in conceiving. If there are no eggs then the woman will never conceive naturally. IVF can help provide her only chance of motherhood.

"Failure to ovulate is the cause of infertility in about three in ten cases. In some women this is a permanent problem. In some women it is intermittent when some months ovulation occurs and some months it doesn't."

Private Healthcare UK – website advising infertile couples about the causes of infertility

Some women who have had families of their own are prepared to act as egg donors. This means they allow eggs to be collected from their ovaries and given to other, infertile women. A donated egg can be fertilized by sperm from the man and placed in the infertile woman's body to develop.

However, in many women who do not ovulate the cause is easier to deal with. Some women don't make enough FSH to stimulate the release of the mature eggs from the ovary and others don't make any at all. Synthetic (laboratory-created) hormones can be used that will replace natural FSH, bringing about ovulation and so, hopefully, pregnancy (see page 16).

TANGLED TUBES?

The most common female physical problem preventing pregnancy is that the Fallopian tubes are twisted, scarred, or blocked in some way. The Fallopian tubes are inside the body, hidden to human eyes. About 11centimetres (4 inches) long, they lead from the ovaries to the uterus. If the tubes are damaged, this prevents the sperm from meeting the egg and even more importantly, stops the egg, fertilized or not, from travelling along to the uterus. Thirty per cent of female infertility is the result of damaged Fallopian tubes.

Techniques like this hysterosalpingogram help doctors decide whether IVF is necessary. If the Fallopian tubes are damaged, as these are, a normal **conception** is impossible. The uterus is the pale, triangular shape in the centre. The Fallopian tube on the left of the picture is not visible meaning that no dye has passed into it from the uterus. This shows that it is blocked. The tube on the right is damaged.

Damage to the tubes is revealed during an investigation known as a **laparoscopy**, usually combined with a dye test. These tests give a good idea of whether or not the tubes are blocked or if there are any abnormalities in the uterus itself. If there seem to be problems the investigation can be taken further with a hysterosalpingogram. For this a special dye that shows up on X-rays is injected up into the cervix. The dye shows up blockages in the Fallopian tubes on the X-rays that are taken.

Sometimes a technique that involves tiny instruments placed into the Fallopian tubes can be used to try to reopen them, but the technique itself can damage the very delicate tubes. When the tubes are badly damaged or blocked then the only hope of a solution is IVF.

... or an infertile man

When a couple visit their doctor about fertility problems, investigations will be made into the fertility of the man as well as the woman. There are two crucial factors: is the man producing sperm in his semen, and are they normal, healthy, and active? The answer to both of these questions comes from a careful examination of the man's semen.

In normal healthy semen there will be hundreds of millions of sperm. In fact, the lowest number of sperm counted as normal is 20 million sperm per 1 centimetres^3 (0.06 inches^3) of semen! Once the sperm count falls below this level it begins to affect fertility – remember that only one out of every 2,000 sperm will make it from the cervix to the Fallopian tubes. If the sperm count is just a bit below normal there are certain things that the man can do to increase the numbers – all of them very low tech! If the testes get too warm, the level of sperm production falls, so cool showers or baths, baggy underwear, and loose clothing can help to increase the sperm count. Smoking and drinking alcohol are known to lower the sperm count, so reducing or stopping these habits can also help increase sperm numbers. If the count is really low, it gets more difficult.

Using a microscope to view a fresh sample of semen reveals just what state the sperm are in, and how many of them there are.

NUMBERS AREN'T EVERYTHING

The overall sperm count is important, but the ability of sperm to fertilize eggs successfully depends on more than numbers. The motility of the sperm is very important too – in other words, how active are they and how well do they swim? For the man to be fertile his sperm need to have actively lashing tails and around 50 per cent of them must swim forward in straight lines rather than round and round in circles.

Even if a man has lots of active sperm it isn't quite enough to be sure that he is fertile. It is also very important that the semen doesn't contain too many abnormal sperm. Every man produces a certain number of sperm with two heads instead of one, or with two tails, or broken necks. But if the percentage of these abnormal sperm gets too high, then the chances of a successful pregnancy fall. Abnormal sperm do not produce abnormal babies – they simply do not fertilize the egg.

Overcoming male infertility is not easy. Until recently the best hope was for the woman to be treated with healthy sperm given by an unknown donor, often mixed with some of her partner's sperm. However, some of the latest developments of IVF involve using a single normal sperm and injecting it into the woman's egg cell, which is then implanted in her uterus. This exciting new development is leading to potential treatment for almost all men with fertility problems, as the numbers of men who produce no healthy sperm at all is relatively small. It has even been possible to take immature sperm from the testes (which are incapable of fertilizing an egg on their own) and inject the head of the sperm into an egg.

DISCUSS — Should fertility treatment be used to pass on faulty genes?

Until recently men who are affected by the genetic condition cystic fibrosis could not father children. They lack the tube that carries sperm away from the testes. As people with cystic fibrosis often did not live long into adulthood, this was not a problem. But improvements in treatment mean many people with cystic fibrosis now live into their 40s and so having children becomes more of an issue. A combination of new techniques means that these problems can be overcome. A small number of men with cystic fibrosis have been able to father children by having immature sperm removed from the testes and injected into the eggs of their partner. But they will definitely have passed on the faulty cystic fibrosis gene to their children who will at the very least be carriers of the disease. For the individuals concerned it is wonderful that they can have their own child. But is it a good thing for society as a whole?

IS IVF THE ONLY WAY?

The best known treatment for infertility is IVF. It is never far away from the news headlines, not least because of the many new treatments that have followed in its wake. However, when a couple first have fertility problems, treatment will not always involve IVF.

One of the most common ways of treating fertility problems involves fertility drugs. These are not only remarkably successful in their own right, but have also paved the way for the development of IVF. One of the main reasons women fail to get pregnant is because they do not produce mature eggs. Fertility drugs are chemicals that work in different ways to stimulate the woman's body to produce and release a mature egg from the ovary.

DISCUSS Lifestyle and infertility

Some of the most common causes of infertility result from people's lifestyle choices. How much you eat and exercise has a big effect on your chances of a successful pregnancy. But weight isn't the only thing that can cause infertility.

Smokers are more likely to have problems getting pregnant than non-smokers. Smoking seems to affect the ovaries, so women smokers are less likely to ovulate successfully. If they do get pregnant, they have a higher risk of miscarriage or their baby having abnormalities. Men who smoke are more likely to have abnormal sperm that cannot fertilize the ovum. Stopping smoking doesn't solve the problem immediately, but within about three months the reproductive systems are more or less the same as non-smokers. Drinking alcohol can also affect fertility. In women, heavy drinking can disrupt the menstrual cycle and even prevent ovulation. In men, it reduces the quality and number of sperm produced and can also leave a man unable to have an erection, which makes intercourse and conception very difficult. In most cases doctors advise people to change their behaviour – lose weight, gain weight, stop drinking or smoking – as a first stage in the treatment of their infertility. If people can't or won't change their lifestyle, should they be given medical treatment for a problem that is largely of their own making?

"Excess weight reduces your chances of getting pregnant and staying pregnant. Being too thin stops your body producing eggs – so gives you no chance of pregnancy at all."

Dr Richard Howell, obstetrician and gynaenocologist with a special interest in infertility treatment

The most widely used drug is clomiphene citrate. This drug works by fooling the body into making extra FSH and so stimulating the production of eggs by the ovaries. When women do not make any of their own FSH they can be given different drugs that actually contain human hormones. These stimulate the ovaries directly. Other fertility drugs can be used if the mature eggs are not released from the ovaries.

The use of these drugs has been very successful in helping many infertile couples to have children, and it has been vital in the development of IVF. To carry out this technique doctors need to harvest a number of eggs to fertilize outside the body. Even with fertile women, only one or at most two eggs mature enough each month to be released from the ovary. So when doctors are working with their patients towards IVF, fertility drugs are an important part of the preparation.

FOCUS   Three's a crowd?

Fertility drugs have helped many infertile couples to have children, but when they were first developed they caused problems of their own. In the early days of fertility drugs, doctors were not always sure of the doses to use, and many of the women using the drugs had multiple pregnancies – in other words, more than one egg was released and fertilized at the same time. Twins did not cause too many problems, but far more people than expected had triplets, quads, or an even larger number of babies.

Large multiple pregnancies cause many problems. When lots of babies develop in the same uterus, there is a much increased risk that labour will start very early as the uterus becomes hopelessly overstretched. Very tiny babies born at this stage are quite likely to die or become brain damaged. Now, with increased knowledge of the way fertility drugs work and close control of the dosage, large multiple pregnancies can usually be avoided.

These sextuplets are six months old.

THE IVF STORY

For centuries people have tried to overcome infertility by whatever means they had available. Scientists and doctors have trodden a long and difficult path to reach the stage we are at today, with IVF and other treatments holding out the hope of a baby to many who would otherwise be childless. Many aspects of human fertility had to be understood before it became possible to fertilize a human egg outside of the mother's body and return it to her uterus to grow into a full-term, healthy baby.

For many years people had little understanding of how human reproduction worked. For example, a long-held belief was that the man supplied the entire new baby in the head of his sperm (see left), and the woman simply acted as a "super-seedbed", providing the growing child with all that it needed until it was born. Until beliefs like this were overturned by scientific knowledge, any attempts to overcome infertility were doomed to fail.

Exploring ways of treating infertility is not new science. In the 3rd century, Jewish thinkers were discussing whether it was possible for people to become pregnant by accidental **artificial insemination**. By the 14th century, Arabs were using artificial insemination in their horse-breeding programmes. In 1777, an Italian priest began experiments with artificial insemination in reptiles, and in 1785 there was a major breakthrough, when John Hunter, a Scottish surgeon, made his first attempts at human artificial insemination. As a result of his experiments a child was born that same year.

Into the 20th century

The 20th century saw many significant advances in the treatment of infertility. In the early years of the century scientists like the Americans Samuel Crowe, Harvey Cushing, and John Homans began to unravel the complex chemical control of human fertility. They, along with other scientists, discovered, isolated, and identified the hormones made by the pituitary gland in the brain, and by the ovaries and testes.

Towards the end of the 20th century there was a great deal of controversy and debate about IVF and some of the other treatments that have developed from it. However, this sort of debate is nothing new. Assisting couples to have babies using artificial means has always raised strong feelings – even in the early days there were people who were unhappy at what they saw as unnatural interference with nature.

When early reports of artificial insemination using sperm from a donor were published in the British Medical Journal in 1945 there was great debate in the British Parliament. At that time British researchers were the leaders in the field. In 1948, the Archbishop of Canterbury, the most senior clergyman in Britain, recommended that the practice should be made a criminal offence. The government didn't follow that recommendation, although they did say that the practice was "undesirable and not to be encouraged".

In 1949, an Italian, Dr Piero Donini, produced the first human fertility drug, but it took until 1962 before the first baby was born as a result of drug-triggered ovulation. Meanwhile, in 1954, things had moved forward again: there was a report of four successful pregnancies following the use of frozen sperm. In spite of this, it was another 16 years – that is until 1970 – before the use of artificial insemination using donor sperm became an officially accepted treatment for infertility in the UK. By this time the research had spread across the world, and in many countries, including parts of Europe, the United States, and Australia, artificial insemination was accepted and used.

Understanding grows

As the 1960s dawned, doctors and scientists all over the world were learning more and more about different parts of the process of reproduction, and all of this knowledge and understanding was needed before IVF could be developed.

Their knowledge included the use of fertility drugs to regulate the numbers of eggs that matured in the ovary. Developments in the understanding of the ways in which eggs mature and the events of ovulation were also important. As scientists moved closer towards IVF, it became vitally important that the process of fertilization was thoroughly understood. Just as vital was knowledge about the way early human embryos develop in vitro, outside of their natural environment in the body of the mother. It soon became apparent that human embryos could not survive long outside the ideal environment of the mother, and so transfer back to the mother would need to be done within the first few days of fertilization.

Only once all of this knowledge and understanding was in place could scientists take the next steps forward and move towards developing IVF.

 FOCUS **The early development of the human embryo**

How does an embryo develop? Once an egg and a sperm have joined, the two nuclei fuse together. This means that the genetic material of the father is combined with the genetic material of the mother. Once this has happened a new cell with a unique combination of **DNA** has formed. Immediately the cell begins to divide, and about 30 hours after fertilization the developing embryo has two cells. After 40–50 hours each of these two cells has also divided in two and the embryo consists of four cells. In the human body, these divisions take place as the fertilized egg is beginning to move down the Fallopian tube. Cell divisions continue, until there are 16 cells. Eventually, about four to five days after fertilization, a hollow ball of around 80 cells arrives in the uterus, where it implants itself. At this stage the embryo is known as a **blastocyst**. The developing embryo in IVF may be returned to the body of the mother at any stage, from two cells to blastocyst. From then on, the remaining stages of development will take place in the protected environment of her uterus.

Increasingly, IVF clinics are returning the developing embryo to the uterus at the blastocyst stage rather than at an earlier stage, because this is the point that the embryo would naturally arrive in the uterus and implant.

Enter Edwards and Steptoe

The first time a human egg was fertilized successfully outside the female body was in 1969. It was achieved by Dr Robert Edwards, an academic **physiologist** working at Cambridge University. He used human ovaries that had been removed during surgery as the source of the eggs. The eggs needed to be kept in a very special, chemically balanced fluid – they couldn't just be taken out of the body and left in a dish. This first human *in vitro* fertilization took place in a culture medium, which is a mixture of chemicals and water used to culture eggs and developing embryos. This had been used very successfully for the *in vitro* fertilization of hamster eggs during earlier, animal-based research into infertility treatments.

At the same time, Mr Patrick Steptoe, a **gynaecologist** working at the Royal Oldham Hospital, was developing methods of extracting mature human eggs from the ovary by laparoscopy. He could "harvest" eggs, sucking them up from the ripe **follicle** (cell surrounding the egg) at the stage when they could be fertilized. This was brave stuff, because at that time laparoscopy was considered "a dangerous procedure".

The birth of IVF – and Louise Brown

By 1971, Edwards and Steptoe had met and were sharing their ideas and expertise to work towards a successful fertility treatment. They worked on retrieving eggs from volunteers so they could time egg collection to perfection, and on the best culture conditions for maintaining a human egg and an early embryo outside the body – *in vitro*. They did not use fertility drugs to enhance egg development. They simply monitored their patients very carefully and when ovulation appeared imminent (at whatever hour of the day or night) they operated and collected the egg by laparoscopy.

Before long they felt ready to attempt a pregnancy in an infertile volunteer. By 1975, success was on the horizon – a human embryo was replaced successfully in the body of its mother and a pregnancy began. But the excitement was short-lived. The longed-for pregnancy developed not in the uterus of the mother but in her Fallopian tube. This is known as an **ectopic pregnancy**, and it can cause terrible pain and the risk of severe damage or even death to the mother. An operation was carried out to remove the tube, and the embryo with it, dashing the hopes of doctors and scientists alike. It was also a terrible blow to the couple who so desperately wanted a child that they were prepared to act as human guinea pigs in this amazing experiment.

Robert Edwards (on the left) and Patrick Steptoe – the pioneers whose work resulted in the birth of the first IVF baby and gave hope to countless infertile couples.

However, for Edwards and Steptoe success was not far away. They continued their experiments, in spite of growing media pressure and the clamour of groups who were unhappy with their interference in the process of reproduction. In 1977, they removed a single mature egg from the ovary of Lesley Brown, and fertilized it with sperm from her husband. The embryo that resulted was implanted back into Lesley's uterus and to everyone's delight she became pregnant. Finally, on 25 July 1978, Louise Brown was born – a healthy baby girl conceived in a glass Petri dish. This was truly ground-breaking science – and also the end of years of heartache for the Browns. Both Patrick Steptoe and Robert Edwards were present at the birth – they must have been almost as happy as Mr and Mrs Brown! IVF as a way of overcoming infertility had arrived at last.

Louise Brown, the first baby born as a result of fertilization outside the body. The media coined the phrase "test-tube baby" to describe her astonishing conception, and this colloquial term for IVF stuck.

HOW DOES IVF WORK?

The birth of Louise Brown in 1978 was the climax of years of research but it was just the beginning of new infertility treatments. In the years since then IVF has continued to develop in quite spectacular fashion – the techniques have been refined and new treatments added. Within two years, two Australian groups of researchers helped couples have babies through IVF, but they used a rather different technique. They stimulated their patients with fertility drugs to make sure that plenty of eggs were produced. As they had a higher success rate than the British team, it was their methods of egg collection that were widely adopted. Even Edwards and Steptoe later adopted the use of fertility drugs to stimulate the production of more than one egg, a process known as **superovulation**.

IVF offers a way of overcoming infertility for women whose Fallopian tubes are blocked, twisted, or damaged beyond repair, where neither eggs nor sperm can travel along the tubes. The treatment combines the egg and sperm outside the body, and returns the developing embryo to the uterus, bypassing the need for the Fallopian tubes.

If a couple who are infertile because of damaged Fallopian tubes decide, in consultation with their doctors, that a course of IVF treatment is the way forward for them, what can they expect?

Setting out

Almost every couple who undergo IVF treatment receive initial counselling. This is to make sure that they realize that although the treatment offers them the hope of a baby, it in no way guarantees one. The chances of a couple actually achieving a successful pregnancy are no higher – and probably lower – than a fertile couple attempting to get pregnant by natural methods. If they do get pregnant using IVF, then the risk of multiple pregnancy is higher than for a normal couple. Most clinics feel it is very important that their patients realize these facts before they embark on a course of treatment.

IVF clinics vary widely in who they will accept onto their programmes. Couples who seek help are not just those with blocked or damaged Fallopian tubes. Some couples don't get pregnant and there is no clear reason why not. If they have tried all other methods and failed, IVF may offer them a final chance.

Infertility clinics, such as this one in Milan, Italy, need to find out as much as they can about their patients as quickly as possible, so they use medical notes from the doctors who have carried out earlier investigations into the couple's fertility problem. They also need to talk to the couple to find out what they are looking for and if they are likely to be suitable for the treatments on offer.

Age of woman	% of successful pregnancies per cycle using fresh eggs
Under 35	32.6
35–37	27.3
38–39	19.7
40–42	10.8
42+	4

Some clinics are quite picky about who they will allow onto their programmes. For example, they may only accept the younger couples who are more likely to succeed, both to avoid giving false hope to other couples and to keep their "baby per treatment" average as high as possible. The rate of live babies achieved per treatment is one of the most important factors couples look at when deciding which infertility clinic to choose.

Other clinics specialize in the most-difficult-to-treat cases, such as older couples, couples where both partners have infertility problems, and couples who have already had a number of IVF failures. Yet others are relatively unselective. This is why it is important for couples to find out as much as possible about an infertility clinic, to see if it specializes in treatment that is suitable for their particular problem. Figures for the number of successful pregnancies don't always tell the whole story.

Managing IVF

The first important stage of IVF treatment is to make sure that the woman produces a number of good quality eggs. This is brought about by carefully measured doses of fertility drugs. The development of ripe follicles on the surface of the ovary is then monitored. If not many follicles are developing, doctors will not try to collect eggs. Instead they will try again during the next menstrual cycle, giving the woman a higher dosage of drugs.

COR RT OV

This transvaginal ultrasound of a woman shows a normal appearing ovary containing numerous ovarian follicles. Colour flow dopper applied to this image shows the arterial supply to the ovary in red and the venous drainage in blue.

The development of the eggs maturing in the ovaries is monitored using **ultrasound**, which enables doctors to see how many follicles are forming. Blood tests may also be used to monitor levels of a hormone called oestradiol – as the follicles develop, the levels of oestradiol increase. By combining the information from the blood tests and the ultrasound, doctors can build up a very accurate picture of how many eggs are developing in the ovary and when will be the best time to collect them. About 36 hours before the egg collection is due, the woman is given a final injection of yet another hormone, human chorionic gonadotrophin (hCG). This helps to make sure that the eggs are fully mature in their follicles.

Collecting the eggs is another vital and tense stage of the process. If a number of healthy, mature eggs are not collected, the process cannot go ahead. And just because there are ripe follicles in the ovaries this does not necessarily mean the eggs will be collected successfully – harvesting eggs is a tricky and delicate business.

The process is carried out with the woman either sedated or under a general anaesthetic. An ultrasound probe is placed inside the vagina because this gives a better picture of the position of the ripe follicles than a probe on the stomach. A needle is carefully guided through the wall of the vagina into the body cavity next to the ovaries. The point is then carefully manoeuvred into a ripe follicle. The liquid inside the follicle, including the mature egg, is sucked up into a tube connected to a small pot to collect the eggs.

These ova have been harvested for IVF. They will be injected with sperm to fertilize them and the resultant zygotes (fertilized egg cells) will be grown in the lab until they reach an early stage of embryonic development. They will then be implanted into the patient's uterus.

The big moment

Once the eggs have been collected from the woman they are placed in a special liquid that mimics the normal body fluids. Each egg is put into a small dish in an incubator and kept at body temperature. The acidity level (the pH) is also kept the same as the normal body fluids. This is very important so that the eggs continue to develop properly. The male partner then produces some semen, from which samples of very active sperm are taken. These are added to the dishes containing the eggs four to six hours after the eggs were collected – at the time they would naturally have been released from the ovary – and if all goes well with the insemination the process of fertilization begins. This takes about eighteen hours from start to finish and it is then another twelve hours before the first cell division takes place. At this stage a couple will find out if they have actually achieved any embryos.

During IVF we are able to see the actual process of fertilization, that would otherwise be hidden within the Fallopian tubes of a woman's body. The availability of the very early embryo means it can be checked for serious genetic abnormalities before it is replaced in the body of the mother.

The dividing of these embryonic cells continues for several days. After two days they contain four cells, after three days there are eight cells, and after five days the embryo is a hollow ball of cells called a blastocyst. The embryo can be transferred to the woman's body at any of these stages. During this time the health of the minute embryos will be monitored closely by the **embryologist**. Great care is taken that only healthy, undamaged embryos are replaced in the mother's body, and so the dividing cells are regularly observed through a microscope.

"We choose which embryos to replace by looking at their appearance. A good embryo has even cell divisions and the cells aren't forming small fragments. We have a grading system, and the best grades of embryo give the best pregnancy rates. Having said that, we sometimes have embryos with a poor appearance giving rise to healthy pregnancies and equally some beautiful embryos which don't result in pregnancy at all."

Nicola Monk, embryologist, Winterbourne Hospital Infertility Clinic

Embryo transfer

In some ways transferring the embryos to the mother's body is the simplest part of the procedure. The hormonal state of the woman's body a few days after ovulation means that she is ready to receive an embryo. Some embryos – usually two or three – are placed in a very fine tube called a catheter, which is passed up through the woman's cervix to the top of the uterus. This is the normal – and ideal – site for the embryo to implant. The tiny balls of cells are deposited in the uterus. To help improve the chances of pregnancy occurring, it is common to give a woman additional treatment with the hormone **progesterone** after the embryos have been replaced in her body.

At this stage the woman can go home and carry on with her ordinary life. It must be very tempting to simply stay in bed and not move, to try to make sure that the tiny embryos stay where they are meant to be! However, all the research shows that this doesn't make the slightest difference as to whether the embryos implant or not. After all, an embryo normally manages to implant whatever is going on in the life of its mother!

Finding out

For an infertile couple, the two weeks immediately following embryo transfer must seem never-ending. They have to wait until the woman would be due to have a **period** before they find out if she is actually pregnant or not. Of course, if her period starts, then the IVF has obviously not worked. But if the monthly bleeding does not start on the day it is expected then a very sensitive early pregnancy test can show what is happening to the hormones in the body and give either good news or bad.

An ultrasound scan carried out four to six weeks after the embryos are transferred will confirm the successful pregnancy and also give the couple their first glimpse of their longed-for child – or children! This scan provides important information for the IVF team – it shows them if they have definitely been successful and how many babies are expected. It is also enormously important for the couple concerned, who may well find it very hard to accept the fact that they really are pregnant after trying for so long. Seeing a tiny blob, or blobs, on the ultrasound screen, and the beating of a tiny heart, can help to make the situation seem more real.

This is the sight that everyone on an IVF programme longs to see. A positive pregnancy test means at least one embryo has implanted and a pregnancy has begun!

Once an IVF pregnancy has been established, it becomes just like any other pregnancy. The worries and fears that every mother has for her unborn child may well be greater in a couple who have tried desperately for years to become pregnant, but the actual risks are no higher – unless of course they are expecting twins or triplets. Even then, the risks of problems developing in the pregnancy are no worse than for anyone else expecting more than one baby to arrive.

1 Fertility drugs cause many eggs to ripen at the same time.

2 The eggs are collected and placed in a special solution in a Petri dish.

3 A sample of semen is collected.

4 The eggs and sperm are mixed.

5 The eggs are checked to make sure that they have been fertilized and are growing well.

6 When the fertilized eggs have divided to form tiny balls of cells, they are placed in the mother's uterus.

The stages in the process of IVF can be summarized in a diagram like this. It makes it all look so simple, and yet the technology used here has taken years to perfect and it is still a long way from guaranteeing that a successful pregnancy will result.

THE PRICE OF SUCCESS

IVF is a technique that has improved the chances of having a baby for infertile couples all over the world. Thousands and thousands of children have been born as a result of this still relatively new technology. From an initial success rate of well below 5 per cent, couples now have a 20–25 per cent chance of pregnancy when they undergo IVF. The success rate varies according to the clinical problem as well as the age of the woman. This sounds low but it is similar to the chances of a fertile couple achieving a successful pregnancy if they have sexual intercourse at the fertile time of the month.

These are just some of the people that would not have been born without IVF.

The cost of treatment

The chances of successful IVF treatment vary greatly from clinic to clinic and some appear far better at producing live babies from a single treatment. But what does this have to do with cost?

The cost and the way infertility treatment is paid for varies considerably from country to country. In the UK, the National Health Service (NHS) will provide one cycle of IVF treatment to infertile couples who have no children together if the woman is under 40 and has a **BMI** of 19–30. Beyond this single cycle, or if they are not eligible for NHS treatment, people have to pay for IVF. The process costs between £4,000 and £5,000 for the first cycle, although it can be cheaper for later cycles if embryos or eggs are frozen and stored from the first treatment. Many other European countries provide three free cycles of treatment before couples have to pay. In Australia, the cost of a cycle of IVF is around AUS$2,500-4,000 but this is heavily subsidised by the government so patients pay around AUS$1,000 or less per cycle. When people (or societies, in the case of the NHS) are paying out large sums of money on treatments for infertility, they have a right to know that they are getting good value for money. However, raw figures of babies born per treatment can be deceptive.

How many embryos?

One important factor that affects the success rate of IVF is the number of embryos transferred into the body of the woman, which varies from clinic to clinic and country to country. On one hand, the more embryos that are transferred, the greater the chance of a successful pregnancy. On the other hand, there is a greatly increased risk of multiple pregnancies.

Multiple pregnancies – twins, triplets, or more – are known to have a higher risk of things going wrong. They put an immense strain on the body of the mother when she is carrying them, and they are also more difficult for parents to cope with when they are born.

If the number of embryos transferred is not carefully managed, the longed-for arrival of children to an infertile couple can put an almost unbearable strain on them, particularly as they may well have spent much of their savings on infertility treatment. However, if clinics transferred only one embryo to reduce the risk of a multiple pregnancy, they would also reduce the likelihood of pregnancy. Questions such as these need to be weighed up carefully when couples and their doctors are deciding how to proceed with treatment.

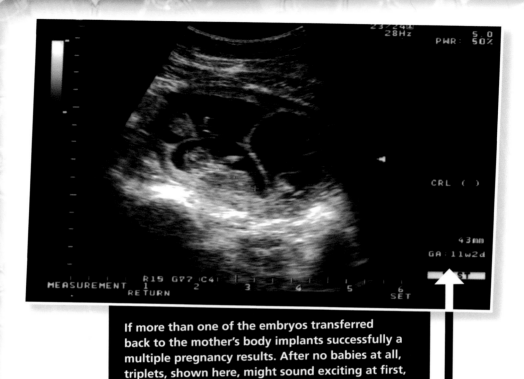

If more than one of the embryos transferred back to the mother's body implants successfully a multiple pregnancy results. After no babies at all, triplets, shown here, might sound exciting at first, but the reality can be very tough.

"*In most cases, replacing more than two embryos does not increase the chance of having a baby but can substantially increase the risk of a multiple birth. There is little benefit in replacing more than two embryos and there can often be considerable physical, emotional, and financial costs.*"

Ruth Deech, Chair of the HFEA

In the UK, under HFEA regulations, a maximum of two embryos can be implanted at any one time, to strike the best balance between giving a good chance of pregnancy with the least risk of a large multiple birth. There are hopes that this will eventually be reduced to one.

In the United States, clinics make their own decisions but in 2006 the American Society for Reproductive Medicine and the US Society for assisted Reproductive Technology issued guidelines recommending that no more than two embryos are transferred at a time to women under 35 and that clinics should consider transferring only one. As women get older, the recommendation is that more embryos should be transferred, up to five at a time in women over 40.

In Australia, the recommendation from the Fertility Society of Australia is for two embryos only to be transferred at a time, with a move to implanting just the single, best embryo in women under 40.

As techniques improve, doctors can achieve similar pregnancy rates using fewer embryos, which is better for the health and well being of both the mother and the baby.

DISCUSS   Does doctor know best?

In 2007, a team at Guy's Hospital in London led a study into a new IVF technique. They showed that growing embryos in culture for five days (instead of the usual three) means the embryos are much more likely to implant successfully and so only one embryo need be transferred to the mother each time. Progress like this is welcomed by scientists and doctors, who want to cut the multiple birth rate that occurs in approximately one out of every four IVF pregnancies. Yet anxious patients, desperate to have a child, often want as many embryos as possible implanted. They are prepared to risk the problems of a multiple pregnancy in their quest to have a child. In the United States, where people pay for their treatment, the multiple birth rates are particularly high. This is a dilemma for the doctors. It seems to make sense that the more embryos implanted, the better the chance of a baby. But this isn't always the case, and the aim of fertility treatment is to produce a single healthy baby. The dilemma is to convince the would-be parents that the doctors really do know best. What do you think?

DORIVER AND IAN'S STORY

Infertility involves real people. The treatments can be messy, time consuming, and are not always successful. So what is infertility treatment really like?

Doriver and Ian Lilley got married when Doriver was 20. Six years later they decided to start a family. But things didn't go quite as planned. After 18 months, Doriver still wasn't pregnant so the couple went to see their doctor. They were lucky – because they had already been trying for a baby for some time, and they had a sympathetic doctor, they were referred quite quickly to an infertility specialist.

None of the initial tests showed any reason why Doriver and Ian were not getting pregnant, yet nothing they tried actually worked. Even when they tried the fertility drug Clomid, nothing happened. All of the treatments that sound so effective in theory did not have the desired effect on the reproductive systems of Doriver and Ian.

"Every time something fails, infertility becomes harder to deal with, as you begin to realize it might not work – ever."

Doriver Lilley

When Ian and Doriver Lilley got married in 1985 they expected to spend a few years enjoying themselves and saving before settling down to family life. But things didn't quite work out …

Infertility takes over

For both Ian and Doriver, being completely out of control of the situation was an alien, and very unpleasant experience. Not conceiving made Doriver feel a failure, and it was very hard having to rely on other people for such a very intimate and personal thing as having a baby. And so far, even science had failed them.

By this stage their NHS doctors felt there was little chance they would succeed in becoming pregnant – if they wanted to try IVF treatment they would have to pay for it themselves. Doriver was feeling desperate.

Making the decision to begin IVF treatment gave Doriver and Ian a renewed sense of optimism. In everyday life Doriver and Ian felt the "odd ones out", the couple who couldn't have a baby. At the IVF clinic they felt normal – everyone else they met at the clinic was in the same boat.

> *"Everyone else seemed pregnant. I kept going in to work, but it was so hard to keep appearing cheerful. Every day when I got home, I'd break down and cry because I couldn't cope with it …"*
>
> Doriver Lilley

In theory, IVF should be a straightforward solution, but when living systems are concerned science and technology sometimes come unstuck.

Will IVF be the answer?

The first treatment was exciting. Doriver's eggs were harvested – in itself an exciting victory – and some healthy embryos were formed and transferred back into her body. They even had a very weakly positive pregnancy test – but the embryos did not implant properly, the levels of pregnancy hormones dropped, and the pregnancy ended just a few days later. In spite of the disappointment Doriver was encouraged, because they had got eggs and they had got embryos. The second attempt was a crushing blow. It failed completely. Things looked bleak.

Doriver and Ian came into a small amount of money and immediately enlisted for their third attempt at IVF. Eggs were harvested, healthy embryos formed, and transferred into Doriver's uterus – and the waiting began. This time the pregnancy test was strongly positive – at least one embryo had definitely implanted in the uterus wall.

> *"I knew that statistically our chances were getting less and less each time we tried – but I also knew that as long as we had any money to spend I was going to keep on trying."*
>
> Doriver Lilley

Steve Green is an embryologist, one of the team at the CARE clinic at The Park Hospital where Ian and Doriver went for treatment. His role was to make sure that the embryos that were replaced in Doriver's uterus were healthy and growing well.

Pregnant at last!

At 32 years old, after 6 years of trying, Doriver was finally pregnant!

Six weeks passed with no problems before Doriver and Ian went for their first ultrasound scan, and when it showed two little embryos growing, they were completely bowled over. Not only were they pregnant, they were expecting twins!

> *"There was a huge pressure to provide good quality sperm. Doriver had been through so much, everything was ready and waiting, she was in theatre and then it all hinged on my one involvement!"*
>
> Ian Lilley

After the twins were born Doriver had little time to marvel at how they had arrived. Caring for newborn twins is enormously time-consuming and tiring – but this was what all the trying and waiting had been about. During infertility treatment the focus is on getting pregnant – it can be easy to forget that at the end of a pregnancy there are babies that grow up into children to look after.

> *"After embryo replacement I did everything in the house and got all our meals ready etc. I know that you are told it doesn't make any difference [what you do in your daily life], but after so long we were not going to take that chance."*
>
> Ian Lilley

> *"Even when I was in labour, when I went into hospital, I kept thinking 'This is it, this is when I'm going to lose them.' I just couldn't believe we were really going to have children of our own."*
>
> Doriver Lilley

> *"When I saw my son being born and I could see his face start to emerge I couldn't believe I was finally to meet my children after so long."*
>
> Ian Lilley

Fate had another twist in the tail – because just when Doriver was planning to return to work she found she was pregnant again, without any artificial intervention. Doriver and Ian were shocked – once again the unpredictability of human fertility had thrown their carefully made plans into disarray. Science has definite limitations – it had been unable to explain their infertility and now science could not really explain their new-found fertility. But once they had got over the shock, there was excitement all round when James made his entry into the world. They thought about contraception – but not before Thomas was on the way. Finally, before their fifth child, Ruthanne, was born, Doriver and Ian took steps to make sure that they wouldn't have any more children! From childlessness more than 12 years ago, Doriver and Ian are now the happy, proud, exhausted, and somewhat bemused parents of five lovely, healthy children!

Doriver and Ian with their five children. As these children grow up, there will be no way of telling that two of them would not exist if it weren't for IVF technology.

39

BEYOND IVF

The techniques of IVF are constantly being refined and adjusted to find ways of giving the highest possible chance of success to infertile couples. For example, for many years embryos have been transferred at the four- or eight-cell stage. Recent work suggests that transferring the blastocysts (five-day-old embryos) will give better pregnancy rates, because this is the stage at which the embryo would enter the uterus in a natural conception.

A number of other new technologies have been developed that help to overcome even more infertility problems. Most of these also involve embryo transfer.

Donor eggs

One of the ways in which IVF has moved forward is in the use of **donor** eggs. It has been shown that if a couple are having trouble conceiving and the woman is over 40, it may be necessary to use an egg donor to achieve a successful pregnancy. In these cases IVF is much more successful when the eggs of a younger woman – less than 37 years old – who is already known to be fertile herself are used. It is not just in couples where the woman at least is older that donor eggs are very useful. Women who have no eggs in their ovaries cannot become pregnant without an egg donor. Also women who carry a genetic disease may need to use donor eggs to avoid passing on a debilitating illness. So the use of donor eggs in IVF, along with donor embryos mentioned earlier, has increased the success rate for older women.

Some doctors use this technology to allow women who are well over the natural age for childbearing to have children. Naturally, a woman passes through the menopause at between 45 and 55 years. At this point she no longer has periods and her ovaries become inactive – no more eggs are released. But by using donor eggs or embryos, women over the age of 50 have been enabled to give birth.

Since the initial breakthrough more than 100 women aged 50 or over have had babies in the United States alone. However, only relatively few clinics will treat older women in this way. There are many people who have real concerns about it, both because of the potential risks to the health of the mother and the age gap between the mother and child – although similar arguments are rarely put forward when older men father children naturally!

Is old for women the same as old for men?

It is not that unusual for men to father babies in their 50s, 60s, and even 70s. Charlie Chaplin, Michael Douglas, and Paul McCartney are just a few of the well-known older fathers around. If a man becomes a father when he is older there are generally congratulations and people are impressed. If a woman becomes a mother when she is older people tend to throw up their hands in horror and she is accused of being irresponsible and putting the child at risk of being an orphan. Yet statistics clearly show that men generally die sooner than women – so late dads are more likely to die and leave their children than older mums. Why is there this difference in attitudes – is it fair or right? Surely both should be congratulated, or both censured. Is this an area where sexism is still alive and well?

Adriana Ilieascu was 66 when she gave birth to her daughter in 2005. Artificial hormones were used to prepare her uterus, and once the pregnancy was established her body took over and maintained it just like a younger woman. Amazingly, she is not the oldest person to give birth. A Spanish woman had twins in 2006 days before her 67th birthday!

A frozen harvest

When the ovaries are encouraged to superovulate they can produce up to twelve ripe eggs in one cycle. These eggs are fertilized and a small number of healthy embryos are then transferred back into the uterus of the mother. However, there may well be other healthy embryos remaining in their dishes. What is to be done with them? Most IVF clinics now offer embryo freezing and storage to their clients. The early embryos are frozen and stored in flasks of liquid nitrogen.

Human sperm have been frozen and stored for years, and frozen animal embryos have been transported around the world for some time, but using frozen human embryos is recent. It seems a dramatic treatment for such delicate tissue.

This has many advantages. If the first attempt at IVF fails the couple can have at least one, if not more, attempts without having to go through the whole process of egg collection again. If, on the other hand, the first attempt is successful, then the remaining embryos can be kept so that if the couple decide they would like another child, they have embryos ready to go. However, the presence of these frozen embryos does raise some questions. One of the simplest is – what happens to the embryos once a couple decide their family is complete?

The embryos may simply be destroyed, but this is not the most usual fate for them. If the parents are willing – and they often are – the embryos may be used for further research into the treatment of human fertility. They may be allowed to continue developing until they are 14 days old – all research on older embryos is banned in most countries. Another alternative is that one couple may donate their "spare" embryos to another infertile couple who cannot produce healthy embryos. Many other couples decide to keep their frozen embryos "just in case" – although most clinics put a limit on the number of years they will keep the embryos before disposing of them. This is not a callous gesture – no-one knows for sure the effect of long term freezing on the future health of the children who might grow from the embryos.

Zoe, the first baby grown from a frozen embryo, was born in Australia in 1984 and suffered no ill effects from her time in the deep freeze!

FOCUS A frozen embryo dilemma

In 2007, Natallie Evans lost her fight to be allowed to have her frozen embryos implanted. Natallie and her partner both underwent IVF treatment to create six embryos prior to Natallie receiving treatment for cancer that would make her infertile. Natallie and her partner later separated. Following the cancer treatment, Natallie's only chance of having her own biological child lay in these six embryos. By law, both parents would have to give consent for the embryos to be returned to her body. Natallie's ex-partner refused. He said he did not want to be a father and requested that the embryos be destroyed. Natallie fought the case right through to the European Court of Human Rights, but she was not allowed to use the embryos. Do you think this was the right decision?

"I am distraught at the court's decision. It is very hard for me to accept the embryos will be destroyed."

Natallie Evans

Life after death?

Another scenario that must be considered is if both parents die in an accident before they have successfully had children. If there are still healthy frozen embryos, should they be implanted inside a surrogate mother and brought into the world to inherit their parents' belongings?

In all of these debates the welfare of the potential children has to be paramount. It could be extremely damaging for children to feel that they had been pawns in their parents' divorce settlement or brought into being to make sure money stayed in the family.

In theory, frozen embryos could be kept for around 10,000 years before the natural background radiation of the earth damaged their DNA to the extent that they would not grow and develop properly. In practice, in the UK there are legal limits – frozen embryos can only be kept for five years, with another five years extension possible if the parents want more time to decide if they want to add to their family. This gives a total of ten years embryo storage. As no-one knows for certain how long frozen embryos can really be stored safely this limit attempts to protect children who might be born damaged in some way from eggs that had been stored for longer than 10 years. Other countries have less strict laws and regulations about this. This again raises child welfare issues, making it possible for one sibling to be thirty or even forty years younger than the other. But whatever the legal situation, the existence of frozen embryos raises difficult issues.

FOCUS   Is freezing eggs a better way?

In the past, although sperm and embryos could be successfully frozen for later use, scientists could not freeze human eggs. Now it is hoped that problems like Natallie's (see page 43) will become a thing of the past as new techniques mean eggs and slices of ovarian tissue can be frozen and stored. This means women who have to undergo cancer treatment can store eggs for when they are ready to have a baby, and the choice of using the eggs will be theirs alone. However, some women want to freeze their eggs so they can concentrate on their careers when they are young and have a baby using their own eggs later in life. Is this an ethical use of the technology?

Injecting sperm – a major breakthrough

Until recently there was no help for couples where the male partner did not produce fertile sperm, apart from artificial insemination by a donor. Recent developments have changed all that, and there are now techniques available that mean it is possible, in theory at least, for almost any man to father a child.

The main technique used is known as ICSI. This stands for Intra Cytoplasmic Sperm Injection. Eggs are harvested from a woman after treatment with fertility drugs in the same way as for IVF. A single sperm is then injected into the **cytoplasm** of each egg cell. The fertilized eggs are then observed as they divide to form early embryos. Two or three healthy embryos will then be returned to the body of the mother just as in normal IVF treatment.

> "ICSI technology has revolutionized the treatment of male factor infertility. This is considerable, because we now appreciate that male factor infertility is probably the single largest cause of infertility amongst couples."
>
> Dr Simon Fischel, CARE clinic, The Park Hospital

ICSI involves injecting a single sperm into the centre of an egg cell so that fertilization can take place. This removes all the normal barriers to conception as the sperm cannot fail to reach the egg.

The first ICSI-produced baby was born in 1992. It is now widely used and is chosen as the best treatment for at least 30 per cent of all the couples who need IVF technology.

The steps in the ICSI procedure are shown below. This process offers two groups of patients the hope of a successful pregnancy: firstly, men who have very few healthy sperm or who cannot produce semen at all, as it only takes one sperm to fertilize each egg; secondly, couples who produce healthy eggs and sperm for IVF but cannot achieve fertilization. This can be overcome by the direct insertion of a sperm into an egg.

1 Eggs are collected from the woman after she has had fertility drugs (to provide lots of eggs).

2 Sperm is collected from the man.

3 Sperm is examined under a high-power microscope, and healthy ones are selected and drawn into a fine pipette (glass tube).

4 Again under the microscope, a single healthy sperm is injected into each egg.

5 Any healthy embryos formed are returned to the body of the mother to develop.

Diagnostic testing

Another development that has led on from the development of IVF is the testing of embryos before they are transferred back to their mother. There are a number of devastating diseases that are the result of problems in the genetic material in the nucleus of the cell. In a process known as preimplantation diagnostic testing, a single cell is removed from the early embryo (this causes it no harm). Scientists can then analyse the DNA from the cell to see if there are any genetic abnormalities. Only healthy embryos will be transferred back to the mother. Some genetic diseases only affect boys, so in this case all that is needed is to identify female embryos for transfer. In other cases the testing is more specific. Parents who have already had a child affected by one of the severe genetic diseases, such as muscular dystrophy, are now offered the chance of this early testing.

DISCUSS: Sex selecting and saviour siblings – are they acceptable?

The ability to tell the sex of an embryo before it is transferred to the uterus raises the issue of sex selection. Some people, for cultural or religious reasons, feel a need to have a son. Other couples desperately want a girl or a boy to make their family complete. Should they be allowed to pay for genetic testing and only chose embryos of the "right" sex?

Sometimes a child has a genetic illness and needs a bone marrow or umbilical cord blood transfusion to save its life. The donor must be the right tissue match and a brother or sister is most likely to provide it. If the parents want another child, they may request preimplantation genetic testing so that their new child is not only disease-free but also a tissue match for their existing, ill child. These genetically selected babies are known as saviour siblings. Many people find this acceptable, but others disapprove, because the unwanted embryos are destroyed. What do you think?

ETHICS, ISSUES, AND THE LAW

The new reproductive technologies from IVF onwards have brought great happiness to millions of couples who have been enabled to have children around the world. However, they have also raised many different issues that people as individuals and society as a whole need to consider. Some of the issues are very practical, and are the direct result of IVF technology.

> *"When making decisions about infertility treatment you have to consider the MEEF equation: Medical issues + Ethical issues + Emotional issues + Financial issues = Treatment."*
>
> Mr Michael Dooley, consultant, Winterbourne Hospital Infertility Clinic

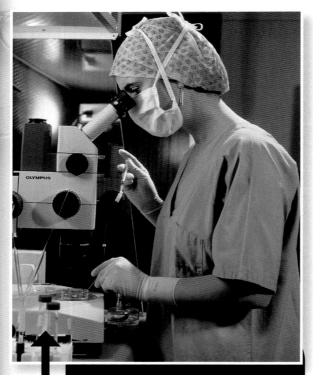

Research on embryos raises people's emotions, whether they are for or against it. But while it is legal the research will continue, and infertile couples and couples with genetic diseases will benefit from the results.

Embryo research

The use of embryos for research is a very sensitive issue. Without embryo research, infertility treatment would never have reached the point it has today. Further steps forward, widening the net of people who can be helped to have a child, depend on more research. Yet this research is carried out on tiny clusters of cells, some of which might, if transferred into a woman's body, turn into babies. For some this is very difficult to accept, and there are groups of people in every country in which this type of research is carried out who object to it very strongly.

Surrogate mothers

The ability to fertilize eggs outside the body has paved the way for another controversial form of infertility treatment – the use of a **surrogate mother**. Some women have ovaries that work perfectly well but do not have a uterus, whilst other women have no reproductive organs at all. Their only chance of having a baby apart from adoption is if another woman will carry a baby for them. This might involve IVF, with embryos from one couple transferred into the uterus of another woman, or it might involve artificial insemination of the surrogate mother with sperm from the father. Whatever the method, the baby grows and develops inside the surrogate mother, who then hands the baby over to its parents very shortly after birth.

There are all sorts of problems with surrogacy. In the UK and Australia it is legal but there can be no payment given to a woman for carrying another person's child. In the United States it is legal but is carried out for money by a number of very successful businesses. The biggest problem is if the surrogate mother decides she cannot hand over the child. There have been legal battles between biological and surrogate parents; in the first test case in the United States, the "purchasing" parents were granted custody of the child, whilst the surrogate mother was granted visiting rights.

At 54, Rebecca Tejwani (left), lovingly volunteered to be a surrogate mother for her daughter Sapna Signh (right). They are seen here with newborn Syrus Sunny.

The law

With the arrival of new technologies there have been legal problems. When dealing with potential human life the risks are great, and different countries have set about dealing with them in different ways. The first concern in most legislation is the welfare of any potential children born using new technology. If there is concern that the health or well-being of the babies conceived might be affected by the technology then most countries are unhappy about its use.

IVF began in the UK, and the UK responded to this giant step forward with a regulatory body known as the Human Fertilisation and Embryology Authority or HFEA. Set up in 1991, the HFEA makes sure that all clinics offering IVF and other infertility treatments in the UK meet strict standards. They collect information about success rates, and

When people wish to change the law they often stage a protest, like these people here. Attempts to change national law in Australia to allow states to ban IVF for single people sparked off such protests.

provide information to the public. The HFEA also licence and monitor all embryo research, supervising what is going on and balancing what should and should not be done. Decisions are made by the 21 members of the authority, who are experts in relevant fields. To make sure that a wide spectrum of views are heard, more than half of the team are not involved in medicine or human embryo research.

So in the UK, things are relatively straightforward. If a treatment is allowed by the HFEA it goes ahead; if it is not, it doesn't.

There is no national legislation in Australia on fertility treatment. However, individual states vary in that some have legislation and others do not. For example, Victoria wanted to prevent single people from receiving IVF treatment. This caused an uproar among the gay community, because two people of the same sex cannot legally marry in Australia. This means that any lesbian woman wanting to have a child is classified as single and so would be unable to have fertility treatment. In response to the outcry commonwealth law was used to stop the state law in 2000.

> "The first IVF baby was born in the UK and we were the first *statutory* government body to regulate this treatment and remain one of the few to do so. While the number of couples seeking IVF treatment rapidly increases we aim to assure a high standard of care and medical expertise whether that clinic is private or public, big or small."
>
> Ruth Deech, HFEA chairperson

In the United States there is a similarly fragmented situation. There are few laws controlling what techniques or research may or may not be carried out. However, legislation compelling medical insurance companies to pay for IVF treatment is being introduced in an increasing number of states, making IVF and other treatments available to more and more couples.

Evidence shows that in states with legislation in place, the number of high risk multiple pregnancies as a result of infertility treatment is much lower than in states where people have to pay for themselves. Naturally, when people desperately want children but have limited funds they will request as many embryos as possible be transferred to try to reduce the number of treatment cycles needed. With no national legislation to limit embryo numbers, some doctors will go with the patients' wishes rather than recognised best practice. But this carries risks for both mothers and babies. There are campaigns in the United States to try to ensure that all states put legislation for insurers to cover infertility treatment in place, to prevent problems like these in future.

A matter of faith

The decisions a couple make about infertility treatments may be affected by their religious beliefs. There is no single view within the different faiths about the acceptability or otherwise of infertility treatments such as IVF. This means that one couple may undergo IVF certain in the belief that it is acceptable, whilst another couple, equally desperate to have a child, may feel unable to accept IVF.

THE ANGLICAN VIEW

The views of the Anglican Church have strong foundations in a belief in marriage and the family and in respect for human life. Therefore the Church does not object in principle to fertility treatment that involves reopening the Fallopian tubes or the use of fertility drugs. Artificial insemination with the husband's sperm is also seen as universally acceptable. However, IVF itself raises more of an issue for some theologians, who see it as a way of improving on nature rather than helping it and therefore as an attempt to "play God". Many other Anglican theologians see the process as a perfectly acceptable way of enabling married couples to enter into the blessing of family life.

The Anglican Church is more concerned about the use of donated eggs, sperm, or embryos, because it can be argued that by bringing a third party into the relationship the marriage vows are broken. The most liberal view accepts any fertility treatment carried out with due reverence and faith, whilst the most conservative view is that any intervention such as IVF is wrong.

THE CATHOLIC STANDPOINT

The teaching of the Catholic Church on infertility treatments is strict and is the same in every country. In 1987, the Pope made the Catholic position very clear in a document called *Donum vitae* ("Respect for life"). He said that treatments such as IVF are not acceptable because they separate the conception of a child from the sexual act between the parents. The Catholic Church also rejects completely any infertility treatment that involves donated eggs, sperm, or embryos as gravely immoral because of the introduction of another person into the marriage bond.

A MUSLIM PERSPECTIVE

Within Islam the production of children is a vitally important part of married life. Islamic teaching also states that for every illness there is a cure, so it is regarded as acceptable and right that an infertile couple should seek help. Treatments such as fertility drugs and procedures to open up the Fallopian tubes are quite acceptable. Islamic scholars also

For many people the spiritual dimension of their lives – their religion – is important in guiding their decisions about fertility treatments.

accept the use of IVF, but only if enormous care is taken that only the eggs and sperm of the husband and wife concerned are used in the treatment. But, as in many other religions, the use of donated eggs, sperm, or embryos is seen as completely unacceptable because it breaks the unity of the marriage bond.

THE JEWISH APPROACH

As in so many other religions, the family is very important to the Jewish faith. Orthodox Jewish law finds assisted reproduction acceptable in helping a Jewish couple to conceive a child as long as the eggs and sperm come from the parents themselves. So IVF using sex cells from the parents is acceptable, and there is often a **rabbinical** supervisor present to make sure that the eggs and sperm are not contaminated by material from non-Jews. But the use of donor eggs or sperm is much less acceptable, and certainly not allowed if the sex cells are not from Jewish people.

THE HINDU APPROACH

For Hindus, with their beliefs in reincarnation and caste (inherited social status), treatments such as IVF raise many problems. Only a husband is allowed to touch his wife, so a doctor cannot intervene in the act of conception, and fear of caste contamination makes donor eggs and sperm unacceptable to strict Hindus.

WHERE DO WE GO FROM HERE?

Some of the most exciting but controversial developments in bioscience and medicine at the moment come as off-shoots of IVF treatments. They include cloning, **genetic engineering**, and **stem cell** research.

Cloning ...

Cloning mammals involves making an identical copy of an adult animal. The nucleus of an adult cell is placed in an empty egg cell. The early embryo that develops is transferred to a surrogate mother to develop. Cloning has been successful in animals such sheep, cats, horses, and even monkeys.

People are now wondering if and when the cloning of people will take place. IVF would make it possible, because the cloned cell would have to be transferred to a uterus to develop into a baby. However, many people are suspicious: will rich and famous people try to clone themselves to become immortal, or will another Adolf Hitler try to use such technology along with genetic engineering to produce a "master race" of people? In some countries it is illegal to attempt to clone a human being, but in others some scientists are already planning to try to produce the first human clone. They feel it will help overcome the problem of infertility – if an infertile woman can give birth to a clone of her partner or herself it would remove the need to use donor sperm or eggs, which can be in short supply and cause religious problems.

This foal, born in 2005, is the first horse clone. Pieraz, winner of two endurance world championships, was cloned by an Italian company in an attempt to preserve the genetic heritage of the champion.

... and genetic engineering

Scientists can change the genetic material of an organism in a process known as genetic engineering (or genetic modification). This has been done successfully in many organisms from bacteria to mice and sheep. Now scientists are trying to replace faulty genes in people affected by genetic diseases with healthy genes, with little success so far. However, the most exciting and most challenging possibility is to change the DNA of an embryo formed outside the body. If faulty genes can be replaced with healthy ones before the embryo is transferred back to the mother, all of the cells of the baby would contain healthy DNA. The genetic disease would be cured, and no longer passed on. But this raises huge ethical questions. If the genes can be changed to cure disease, would some people want to engineer their embryos to be clever, or tall, or beautiful? It is certain that one day it will be possible to genetically engineer human embryos – but will it ever be acceptable?

Down's syndrome is one of many inherited genetic disorders. For some families with these conditions, genetic screening and IVF offer ways of ensuring that their children are free from the disease. However, some couples feel they cannot use these methods because it is against their faith.

Spin-off technology

In 1998, in a breakthrough that caused ripples of excitement through the scientific and medical world, two American scientists managed to culture human embryonic stem cells that were still capable of forming almost all cell types. One team took their cells from spare embryos that had been produced during IVF fertility treatments and donated by the parents for scientific research rather than being destroyed. The other team took human embryonic stem cells from foetuses that had been aborted at 5–9 weeks of gestation.

There was enormous excitement in the scientific world about this breakthrough. In theory at least, these embryonic cells could be encouraged to grow into almost any different type of cell needed in the body. This raised the hope of cures for diseases such as Parkinson's and Alzheimer's, the repair of spinal injuries, new heart muscle cells to repair hearts damaged by heart attacks, and new and effective treatments for strokes, burns, and arthritis. Scientists even hope that embryo stem cells might eventually be used to grow whole new organs for all the people waiting desperately for a transplant.

At the moment no-one is quite sure just how the cells in an embryo are switched on or off to form particular types of tissue – kidney rather than liver, or liver rather than heart. As the answers to these questions are found, the potential will be there for a limitless supply of new organs. Not only that, but the problem of rejection could be solved. The immune system does not attack and destroy a developing embryo even though it has different **antigens** on its cells to the mother. Perhaps new cells or organs created from embryo stem cells will enjoy this same protection.

DISCUSS The ethical stumbling block

The major ethical problem with research using embryonic stem cells is that they come from spare embryos in fertility treatment. Many people, including many religious groups, feel it is wrong to use a potential human being as a source of material in this way. It is also argued that the embryo cannot give permission so using it is a violation of its human rights. In the UK there was considerable debate before legislation was passed to extend the Human Fertilization and Embryology Act to allow embryonic stem cell research to take place. State funding for research into embryonic stem cells was blocked in the United States. After considerable debate the US government decided that from August 2001 such work could continue on the cells as long as rigid criteria were observed.

The use of embryonic stem cells from the umbilical cord of newborn babies may help to overcome some of the reservations. It may become possible to store stem cells from every newborn baby ready for when they might need them later in their lives. Scientists are also finding stem cells in adults that appear to have the ability to grow into several different types of tissue. There seem to be more limitations with adult stem cells than with embryonic ones, but this is another possible way forward, which could avoid both rejection problems and the controversial use of embryonic tissue. Most recently scientists have found a way of reprogramming adult skin cells that makes them revert to stem cells. Again this removes many ethical issues but raises some major scientific stumbling blocks.

Into the future

The future of infertility treatments looks bright. The techniques are being refined and improved all the time, and the numbers of people who have a child through IVF or related treatments continue to grow. Hundreds of thousands of IVF babies are alive today, children who would not exist without the miracle of ground-breaking scientific techniques that allow eggs to be fertilized outside their mother's body. The benefits to the individuals concerned are immeasurable and society also benefits from the birth of more children free from genetic diseases.

However, there are two sides to every story and many people are questioning the acceptability of some of the treatments now being suggested, such as cloning and the use of spare embryos for the development of medical treatments. However, the clock cannot be turned back: we cannot return to the situation before these treatments were discovered, nor would most people wish to do so. The development of IVF and other treatments will continue for the foreseeable future, fulfilling an ever-growing demand, and the debate within society will continue alongside it.

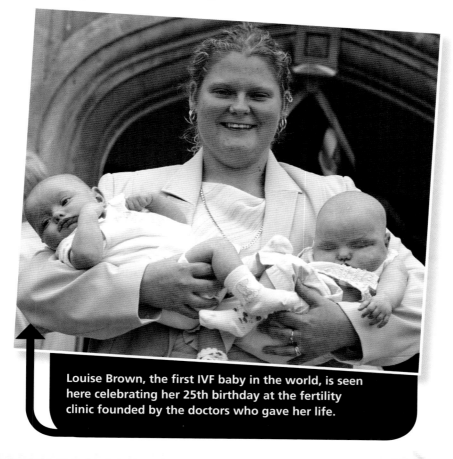

Louise Brown, the first IVF baby in the world, is seen here celebrating her 25th birthday at the fertility clinic founded by the doctors who gave her life.

TIMELINE

200 AD
▲

Records show Jewish thinkers discussing the possibility of accidental or unintentional artificial insemination.

1954
▲

Four successful pregnancies take place using previously frozen sperm.

1949
▲

Dr Piero Donini, an Italian, produces the first human fertility drug.

1945
▲

Early reports of artificial insemination using donor sperm published in the British Medical Journal.

1960s

Rapid increase in understanding of the female reproductive system and the process of fertilization. Drugs are developed that stimulate ovaries so they produce eggs, and laparoscopy methods are improved, making the treatment safer.

1962
▲

First baby born as a result of drug-triggered ovulation.

1969
▲

Human fertilization in vitro is achieved for the first time.

2001
▲

Teams in the United States and Italy announce that they are working on producing the first human clone.

A French woman of 62 who wants a child to inherit her property and money has a baby through IVF, using sperm from her brother and a donated egg.

1998
▲

Growing embryonic stem cells in the laboratory opens the way for different types of cells and organs to be grown as needed for use in transplant surgery. Some of these stem cells come from "spare" embryos donated by a couple who have had successful IVF treatment.

2004

Guidance in UK that all infertile couples meeting criteria of age and body mass index entitled to one free cycle of IVF treatment.

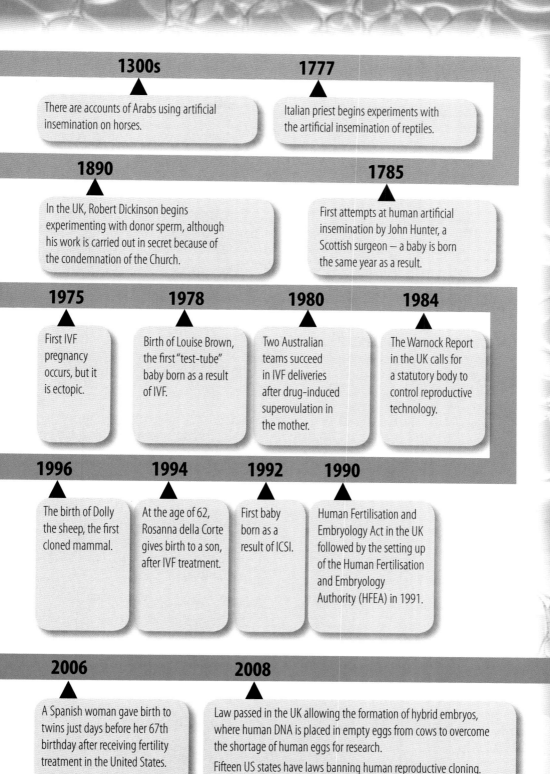

1300s

There are accounts of Arabs using artificial insemination on horses.

1777

Italian priest begins experiments with the artificial insemination of reptiles.

1890

In the UK, Robert Dickinson begins experimenting with donor sperm, although his work is carried out in secret because of the condemnation of the Church.

1785

First attempts at human artificial insemination by John Hunter, a Scottish surgeon – a baby is born the same year as a result.

1975

First IVF pregnancy occurs, but it is ectopic.

1978

Birth of Louise Brown, the first "test-tube" baby born as a result of IVF.

1980

Two Australian teams succeed in IVF deliveries after drug-induced superovulation in the mother.

1984

The Warnock Report in the UK calls for a statutory body to control reproductive technology.

1996

The birth of Dolly the sheep, the first cloned mammal.

1994

At the age of 62, Rosanna della Corte gives birth to a son, after IVF treatment.

1992

First baby born as a result of ICSI.

1990

Human Fertilisation and Embryology Act in the UK followed by the setting up of the Human Fertilisation and Embryology Authority (HFEA) in 1991.

2006

A Spanish woman gave birth to twins just days before her 67th birthday after receiving fertility treatment in the United States.

2008

Law passed in the UK allowing the formation of hybrid embryos, where human DNA is placed in empty eggs from cows to overcome the shortage of human eggs for research.

Fifteen US states have laws banning human reproductive cloning.

GLOSSARY

antigen special marker molecule sticking out from the surface of cell membranes (outer covering of cell)

artificial insemination inserting sperm into the vagina using a device, rather than through sexual intercourse

blastocyst hollow ball of cells formed after the fertilization of an egg

BMI (Body Mass Index) measure of body fat based on height and weight

cervix lower part of the uterus that extends into the vagina

conception fertilization of an egg by a sperm, followed by the egg's implantation in the wall of the uterus

contraception using a condom, contraceptive pill, or other method to prevent the conception of a child

cytoplasm jelly-like substance that fills the cell and in which the components of the cell are suspended

DNA (deoxyribonucleic acid) type of nucleic acid, found in the nucleus of a cell, which carries the genetic code

donor someone who gives an organ or a product of their body – for example eggs or sperm – to help someone who has a faulty organ or product

ectopic pregnancy pregnancy in which the embryo implants and develops in one of the Fallopian tubes instead of in the uterus

embryo term for an egg after it has been fertilized, when it is in its early stages of development

embryologist doctor or scientist who specializes in the study of embryos

enzyme special protein that makes possible or speeds up the rate of chemical reactions

ethics consideration of what is morally right or wrong

Fallopian tube one of a pair of tubes that link the ovaries and the uterus in the female reproductive system

fertility, fertile ability to produce offspring

fertility drugs chemicals that stimulate the development of mature eggs in the follicles of the ovary

fertilization union of egg and sperm that is necessary to produce offspring

follicle cell surrounding the developing egg in the ovary

Follicle Stimulating Hormone (FSH) sex hormone that causes some of the follicles of the ovary to ripen and the eggs within them to mature

genetic to do with the genes, the units of inheritance that are passed on from parent to offspring and determine the offspring's characteristics. Each gene is made from a length of DNA, found in the nucleus of a cell.

genetic engineering process by which the genetic material of a cell may be altered either by replacing damaged genetic material or adding extra genetic material

gynaecologist doctor who specializes in problems of the female reproductive system

hormone chemical messenger made in one place in the body which has an effect somewhere else in the body

ICSI Intra Cytoplasmic Sperm Injection, the injection of a single sperm right into the cytoplasm of each egg cell

in vitro Latin for "in glass" – term used to describe the fertilization of an egg in a Petri dish

infertility, infertile inability to produce offspring

laparoscopy technique for looking at the Fallopian tubes by inserting an instrument into the abdomen

menstrual cycle approximately 28-day cycle of female fertility

mucus slimy substance produced by membranes in some parts of the body

nucleus (plural **nuclei**) central part of a cell, which controls many cell functions and contains a person's DNA

oestrogen female sex hormone made by the ovaries, involved in the release of a mature egg

ovaries pair of female sex organs where eggs are stored and mature, and where the sex hormones oestrogen and progesterone are produced

ovulation release of a mature egg from the ovary

ovum (also known as the egg) female sex cell

period time (usually 5–7 days) in the middle of the menstrual cycle when pregnancy has not occurred and when the lining of the uterus is shed resulting in bleeding; also called menstruation.

Petri dish small shallow dish made from thin glass, traditionally used for studying the behaviour of bacteria

physiologist someone who studies the human body and its functions

pituitary gland small structure in the brain that produces many hormones

progesterone hormone of pregnancy that prevents menstruation from occurring

puberty stage when the body of a child undergoes physical development to become a sexually mature adult

rabbinical concerned with Jewish law

reproduction making of a new individual

semen mixture of sperm and fluids produced by a man when he ejaculates (discharges semen)

sperm male sex cell

statutory having legal authority

stem cell "immortal" cell that retains the ability to divide and multiply and to create other types of cell. Stem cells are found in embryos, bone marrow, skin, intestine, and muscle tissue.

superovulate when women produce many mature follicles containing mature eggs ready for release at the same time

surrogate mother woman who carries a baby for a couple who are unable to have a child of their own

testes pair of male sex organs in which sperm and semen are produced along with the male sex hormone testosterone

ultrasound using extremely high frequency sound waves to produce images of inside the human body. Ultrasound is used for examining developing babies in the uterus.

uterus organ of the female reproductive system in which the baby grows and develops (also known as the womb)

FIND OUT MORE

Further reading

Cutting Edge Medicine: In Vitro Fertilization, Steve Parker (World Almanac Library, 2007)

Library of Sexual Health: Fertility, Michael R. Wilson (Rosen Publishing Group, 2009)

Our Bodies: Reproduction, Steve Parker (Wayland, 2007)

Why Science Matters: Pregnancy and Birth, Ann Fullick (Heinemann Library, 2009)

Websites

The following websites give information on different types of infertility treatment, on the history of reproductive medicine, and how to find the right fertility treatment:

http://www.patient.co.uk/showdoc/23068770/
This website reports on the advice given to people suffering from infertility.

www.repromed.co.uk
Gives information on reproductive medicine, specifically fertility, menopause, and support groups. Also provides details of Bristol University's Centre for Reproductive Medicine, which was established in 1983; the centre does both research and has clinical involvement in IVF treatment.

INDEX